GROUNDING THE CLOUD

Big Data and The Alphabet of Security

by

Todd D. Lyle, MS

ISBN: 0692566945
ISBN 13: 9780692566947

TABLE OF CONTENTS

Foreword

PREFACE

Grounding the Cloud: Big Data and The Alphabet of Security is the second in the Grounding the Cloud series. As in my first effort, Grounding the Cloud: Basics and Brokerages, this book is designed for you to skip around at your leisure depending on your interest in big data and/or your security needs.

In the following chapters you will have the opportunity to learn from real people working at real companies. Their stories will personify words such as data science, analytics, and risk management as they apply to big data and cyber- security. These individuals are leaders in their given organizations; only by staying well ahead of the curve on the newest trends and technologies do they achieve success.

In Grounding the Cloud: Big Data and the Alphabet of Security you will learn all about big data. I will give you a clear definition of the term and discuss what the hype is all about. We'll explore why, after decades of collecting information, big data is only now being recognized as a legitimate force in business. You will discover how much it can benefit your organization, and how you can specifically utilize it.

We will, from A-Z, highlight your personal responsibilities when it comes to internet security and clarify the jargon to give you some ideas of where to shore up your cyber-security measures.

There is a lot of information already in the public lexicon about big data's benefits as well as the expanding need for increased cyber-security. There is also an enormous amount of misinformation out there, with equal numbers of professionals and academics advocating their specific theories and fixes, arguing past one another more often than not.

My ideology tends to take a birds-eye view of current events in order to focus on the single most important variable: the human element.

There are myriad challenges directly connected to the human element with regard to implementing plans for continuity and modernization within any organization. Who is all this new technology supposed to be helping? Humans. Who writes all the code, the algorithms, etc.? Humans. And where does the disconnect most often occur? Exactly. Humans. The larger point being that new technologies or increased security measures don't do much good if your staff isn't adopting/adapting and applying timely counter-measures. Technology doesn't happen in a vacuum. It's not sterile. All of this wonderful new technology that's making our lives easier is created *by* people *for* people. What we all want in the end is full integration and maximum productivity across the board. In order to achieve these lofty goals, we must acknowledge the importance of the human element (i.e. our different abilities, expectations and personalities) as it relates to technology from creation straight through implementation and beyond.

Definitions

Big Data: the aggregation of large amounts of data that can be analyzed for patterns and relationships to discern useful information.

Data Mining: the analysis of large amounts of data for patterns and relationships to discern useful information.

Cloud Security: policies, technologies and procedures used to protect data, applications and infrastructure associated with cloud computing.

Cyber-security: IT security that focuses on protecting computer networks, computer systems, programs, and data that is stored and transmitted over them from unauthorized access, change or destruction.

Cyber Terrorism: when terrorist groups or groups of organized hackers try to further their political agenda by disrupting the use of information technology on computer systems, networks and telecommunications systems.

Cyber Warfare: the fifth-domain of warfare (following land, sea, air and space.) It involves nation-states penetrating information technology, computer systems, and networks of another nation to cause damage and disruption. But, instead of shutting down the nation's networks, the purpose of the attack is to steal valuable data, or degrade and compromise intricate infrastructural systems such as medical and transportation services.

Network Security: policies, technologies and procedures used to protect network equipment and communications from unauthorized access and modification.

Disaster Recovery: a set of policies and procedures that enable technology systems to return to operational status after a man-made or natural disaster led it to shut down.

Machine Learning: the ability of computer systems to make predictions and perform actions based on analysis and aggregate data inputs.

Information Privacy: the ability to protect and restrict access to information collected and stored. It ensures that information is available only to those authorized to access it.

Hacker: anyone with the skill to access a computer system or network without authorization of the owner. Hackers typically exploit weaknesses in system defenses to gain access, disrupt system operations and steal data.

Malware: short for Malicious Software. Software designed to damage or disrupt computer systems, steal sensitive information or grant access to attackers.

Introduction

Without trust there is no continuity. Trust makes the difference between success or failure and life or death.

My first time actually flying an aircraft was in a tiny TH-55 Osage. This particular aircraft is a rather low-tech helicopter, and looks very much like the choppers that were used on the television series M*A*S*H that ran in the 70's and 80's.

It was a beautiful September day in 1987 way down in lower Alabama and I was about to embark on my "nickel ride." As a student pilot, the very first time you actually sit at the controls with a trained instructor and take to the air, that flight is called your nickel ride. The term is born out of the tradition of the student handing a nickel to their instructor once the aircraft is safely on the ground again.

My primary flight instructor back in 1987 was Jerry Irwin, known to all as "Mr. Process," and for good reason. Jerry is very student friendly, but he is also very tough. His attitude is that you have to know all processes and procedures by rote, so that in a high-stress or crisis situation your training takes over and you can handle any scenario. Before becoming a flight instructor at Shell Army Heliport, Jerry had flown combat helicopter missions in Vietnam and had also been a flight instructor for the Shah's Imperial Iranian Army. With a wealth of knowledge, experience, and steely patience, this man kept his student pilots jumping at every turn.

Always stressing the importance of applicable knowledge and process, Jerry was infamous for cutting the engine or creating some other simulated emergency while in the air to see how his students would respond. It was drilled into us how critical it is to keep your head in a crisis, to respond calmly and quickly in times of stress. Lives depended on it. My life depended on it.

One year later at a ceremony at Fort Rucker's Officer's Club Jerry pinned on my US Army flight wings. No longer a "student" pilot, two weeks later I began a UH-60 Blackhawk helicopter transition. I remember sitting down in the right seat of the simulator's cockpit for the first time and being visually and technically overwhelmed. It seemed as if there were 1,000 buttons, switches, fuses, flight controls, and radios. But I was young and like most young pilots, I was cocky. I was going to fly the Blackhawk. Numerous times in my first 30 hours in the simulator I would talk with Jerry about how it seemed so crazy that we were using these highly advanced aircraft in some of the most severe environments. How in the world can you provide mission readiness and maintenance for these incredibly high-tech machines while you're in the middle of a desert, rice paddy or on the side of a mountain?

"Compounded knowledge and trust," Jerry had said. "I've seen it time and again a unified group can do anything."

The first time I was in the front seat of a real Blackhawk helicopter was one month later, and it ended abruptly. At about 100 feet above the ground the master caution light display indicated a right engine fire. Only this time it wasn't a test or simulated emergency. This was the real thing and lives depended on an immediate and very precise interaction between human beings and technology in order to avoid disaster. As the aircraft's systems began their automated commands, I was at the controls while my instructor radioed in our Mayday.

Once the emergency landing checklist was safely completed and after a visit from what appeared to be every fire truck and first responder on duty at Cairns Army Airfield that day, it became clear to me that the potential for loss had been successfully controlled by a team of people utilizing rote memorization and reflex memory to do their job quickly and properly. The immediate response and actions of the entire emergency apparatus at Fort Rucker was an impressive display of teamwork supported by training and advanced technology, processes, and protocols.

To bring the conversation full circle, reacting to online security threats and data breaches is similar to behaving like a pilot in a cockpit. There is a lot that goes into keeping our organizations' data safe today. It is not a one-person show. It requires trust in others, sometimes in an outside unit or in some cases several outside units. Each of these team members or components needs to be doing his or her job and paying attention since attacks on you, your family, or your business can come from anywhere at any time.

Harnessing the power of big data requires a lot more than just looking at statistics and predicting trends. Data is just information compiled. It's static. Success most often is a result of the quality of the team of companies and individuals you have assembled to not just obtain but to analyze the data- a team that works at peak performance when there is a happy union between cutting edge technology and the human element.

Trust, specifically trust in systems and people you don't know - what Jerry Irwin calls compounded knowledge - is absolutely essential to success. In the following pages I will become your "Mr. Process" while pointing out the human element as we relate to every aspect of technology, Big Data and cyber-security. Strap in and enjoy the ride. We've got people to meet, things to learn and plans to implement.

Tech Stuff

What is Big Data?

Unless you have been hiding under a rock, you have heard the term 'Big Data.' Big data has proven itself to be more than just another techie internet buzzword. It has become one of the biggest value-adds in business, if applied correctly.

Prior to the age of big data, we still crunched numbers, but the data was limited to statistics gathered from in-store purchases, credit card transactions, and information obtained from census data along with early polls such as the National Family Opinion poll. However, in the age of omni-present computers, the amount of data available is quickly becoming almost unmanageable.

In the simplest definition, Big Data is the collection and sifting of large amounts of data which can then be analyzed for patterns and relationships to discern useful information. Big data focuses on what we can learn about others in correspondence to specific areas of collected information, and allows that information to be harnessed in order to better serve businesses or individuals. Typically, in a business setting, this data is compiled from your company's database and/or industry research. The more comprehensive data your company has access to, the more you will be able to specifically target your advertising, sales calls, marketing, and much more.

Data itself is currently in a state of mutation. In 2010 only one-quarter of the world's data was stored online. Today, less than 2% of data is left to be converted from paper to electronic. This means there are massive amounts of information ready to be accessed, analyzed, and utilized. The question then becomes: what to do with it?

Data is being put to incredible new uses with the assistance of inexpensive computer memory, high-speed processing, and smart algorithms. With the onset of machine learning, algorithms are beginning to infer. This marks a true transformation in how society and its machines process information, and as a result, copious amounts of 'actionable' data abound.

Business is not the only place that big data will be changing the landscape. It has and will continue to change how healthcare tracks everything from viral outbreaks to routine preventative patient care. In February 2009, Google published a paper in *Nature* that showed how it was possible to track outbreaks of the flu using nothing more than the archived records of Google searches. Wearables such as Fitbit and Jawbone are collecting data including heart rate and pulse. With a licensed practitioner and their coordination this data can help a patient more acutely understand their vital signs. Exponentially, think of the possibilities offered by the availability of real-time big data collections to the medical and research professionals globally as a real-time anthropological study. In the future, big data will provide much needed clarity to tasks that currently require human judgment, such as detecting illnesses or diseases in their early stages.

Big data will become integral to addressing many of the world's pressing problems. Climate change will require analyzing pollution data to understand where best to focus efforts and find ways to mitigate problems. Currently, there are sensors being placed all over the world which provide a massive amount of data that will allow the theory of global warming to be modeled. Big data is already being used to help predict the weather. The Weather Channel monitors over 20 terabytes of data a day, and scientists are actively analyzing this data as you're reading these words to predict natural disasters and save lives. Big data is also being leveraged to combat the 7,000+ U.S. kids that drop out of school every day as trends are being analyzed to learn how teachers can engage more students in the classroom at an earlier stage, before negative patterns begin.

With the enormous benefits big data presents, the challenge is mining usable intelligence and implementing a plan in a timely manner. For this to occur, the big data concept must morph into big data analysis; however the power to gather massive amounts of seemingly disparate bits of information and harness them into neat, organized spreadsheets and dashboards opens the door to a whole new set of challenges. While there is a wealth of potential and value locked in the numbers, understanding and translating that data into something of value is not simple.

In a Western society where data will shape our decisions more and more, how will we know what information applies to us? This is where analytics must take center stage. Many business and IT leaders who were addressing HYPERLINK "http://searchcio.techtarget.com/news/2240164040/Big-data-management-More-like-big-decisions-management" big data management issues just a few years ago are now using HYPERLINK "http://searchfinancialapplications.techtarget.com/feature/Workday-Big-Data-Analytics-helps-Spectrum-mix-HR-and-financial-data" big data analytics to identify trends, detect patterns, and glean other valuable findings from the sea of information available to them. You may be tempted to jump into buying data analytics software, hoping it will be the answer to your company's business needs, but it may take more than a computer program to handle the task. Depending on the scope of your operation, you may need someone to help focus your search, then analyze and explain that data in lay terms.

The single biggest challenge to mining data is focus. You HAVE TO KNOW what you are looking for. It's important to remember that big data is a resource that is meant to inform rather than help explain with conclusion. Therefore, data translation is necessary, and that comes with a cost. Enter the human element. To ensure we are not crowded out by data and machine-made answers, we have humans to direct the focus of your information search, which is already spawning a plethora of new jobs such as data scientist, data analyst, and Chief Data Officer. If your needs are large enough, these professionals can be the filters through which you extract the precise information you want out of big data.

If you decide to utilize big data, do so with an appreciation not just of what it will bring to your business but also its limitations and potential cost. Before investing in big data it is essential to know what you want to accomplish. Many small businesses can continue indefinitely without assistance; either their customer base is small or their target demographics very narrow. For these businesses buying expensive tools to drill down for information beyond your organization's needs and goals is probably not necessary. But for medium to large sized businesses, mining big data is the way of the future.

Points of Interest:

1. Big data is the aggregation of large amounts of data that can be analyzed for patterns and relationships to discern useful information.
2. Big data is quickly becoming an essential tool for business, science, and academia.
3. Due to advances in computer science, the amount of data under review has reached an all-time high.
4. Big data is not simply about raw numbers and technology. There is also a human element involved for an optimal result.
5. Big data is a resource and a tool that is meant to inform rather than explain and there is often a cost associated with it.

What is Cyber-Security?

Cyberspace has become the fifth-domain of warfare following land, sea, air and space. Cyber warfare involves nation-states and rogue terrorists penetrating information technology, computer systems, and networks of another nation to cause damage and disruption. But, instead of shutting down a nation's network, the purpose of the attack is to embed malicious code, steal valuable data, or degrade intricate infrastructural systems such as communications, medical information and transportation services. The other tactic that they commonly utilize falls under the category of cyber espionage. This is when the cyber criminals obtain confidential information without permission from the data holder and use it to gain economic, political, or military advantage. We saw this in 2016 election, when a group of hackers were found to be directly influencing the United States Presidential Election.

While the most disruptive form of cyber threats will take aim at the national infrastructure (critical sectors including power grids, banking & finance - specifically Wall Street and the stock market, and communications including the internet itself - anything that's run by computers), most Americans will at one point or another become victims of hackers, malware, and/or phishing scams and have our privacy compromised or outright stolen. All of that can happen on the internet with just a few keystrokes.

We live in an age of unprecedented communication and convenience, where our money, assets, data and valuables are no longer in a safety deposit box down at the bank or tucked safely away in a fireproof safe under our bed. Instead we have cyber bank accounts with 24-hour online access, electronic mail, text messaging, and Facebook, et al. Long live the internet! It's made a great many tasks in our daily lives infinitely easier, and given us wide open lines of communication with our family, friends, and businesses alike. However, as much as we all appreciate what computers and the internet have done in our daily lives, the inconvenient truth is that the internet is fairly new and so far largely unregulated. This means that we're living in a time in which burglars no longer have to lurk in the shadows and thieves don't have to break the glass in your back door in order to steal from you.

The more confidential data we store on a computer, the more we have to protect. But it's important to note that it's not just individuals that are storing crucial information in cyberspace. It is also businesses, hospitals, financial institutions, the military and our government, and the data stored includes everything from our job histories and medical records to issues of national security. It is no wonder that cyber threats, cyber terrorism, cyber warfare, and cyber espionage have increased seventeen-fold since 2009.

With all of the convenience and simplicity the internet has brought us, most of us never stop to consider just how dangerous cyberspace can be. The direct result is that the majority of Americans don't take the proper steps to protect themselves and their most valuable asset: their cyber persona. Far from being on guard and insistent about our privacy, we openly share everything from financial data, account numbers, and passwords, to our most secret personal information through online commerce, texts, emails, chats, and social networking. And we do it on a daily basis. Sure we try to convince ourselves that we've set up privacy restrictions or firewalls or monitoring systems, but seriously, if the FBI can get hacked, is anywhere safe on the Internet?

With the rampant onset of malware, sophisticated cyber-attacks have drastically increased as has the need for human command, control and coordination. Cyber-security or IT security focuses on protecting computer networks, computer systems, programs and data that is stored and/or transmitted from unauthorized access.

Understanding the enemy is the first step in protecting yourself. There are several different types of cyber criminals out there today and they attack in many different ways. While your business may not be under attack by a large international cyber terrorism group, if you are storing sensitive data or credit card numbers, you may one day find your "protected data" compromised by one or more hackers that will operate remotely using any number of methods that all fall under the broad term we know as malware or malicious software. The type and size of your business drives which cyber criminals you should be guarding against. The smart move is to methodically and patiently prepare for any and all attacks.

The most common term that we hear and fear is the computer virus. When a hacker sends you a computer virus it is meant to gain access, steal, modify and/or corrupt files on your system. A hacker does this by sending out a small piece of software that can replicate itself and spread from one computer to another - much like a virus does in human beings. The most well-known type of malware is Spyware/Adware. This occurs when you click on or download infected software. The spyware will begin to take control of your computer by collecting your personal information to send back to the writer of the software. Worms are another typical malware. They are sent out to damage computer networks and also allow remote control of infected systems. Once they find their way in, they begin to self-replicate and the worm reports back to the worm author to take control. They do not require a program to attach themselves to, making them especially tricky to find.

Another type of malware is a Trojan. A Trojan is a software program that appears to perform one function, such as removing a virus, but actually does something harmful. The Trojan will enter under false pretenses, whether it is an enticing email or a fake website. Once you click to open or download, it will steal your information and even possibly damage your computer.

Cyber criminals implement attacks by way of various types of malware. Phishing is when a virus masquerades as a legitimate entity to attempt to acquire a user's information. Charming is when there is an attack to redirect a website's traffic to email or fake website. The fake website attempts to coax an individual for information, thus compromising the individual. New and more effective methods for cyber criminals to try to cheat users out of their information, data, and financial information are being created all the time.

It is imperative to remember that the simplest way hackers steal your information is by your giving it to them. When it comes to your personal life, a great deal of your online privacy is in your hands. What you share and don't share online is your choice, but once you post something online it is there forever, so it follows that compartmentalizing your information is vital. Understand and be aware that your favorite websites such as Google and Amazon and social networks including FB, Twitter, Instagram and the like are actively collecting and then sharing/selling your information. What privacy rights you have and what each site protects, collects, stores, and shares is different, so when surfing the web, a good rule of thumb is that if you aren't paying for it, someone else is. Thus, your information is being commoditized and is by definition no longer private.

Remember, cyber criminals are indiscriminate. They don't care if you only have a few micro bytes of data or hundreds of terabytes. Whether your data is stored on your own personal network or in the cloud, if there is a weakness, hackers will try to exploit it. For those who have chosen to keep their data off the cloud, there is still a strong need for Network Security. Network security is the policy, technologies and procedures used to protect network equipment and communications from unauthorized access and modification. In order to safeguard data, individuals and organizations need to recognize the threats they are under and how to best safeguard themselves, their customers, and intellectual capital. Whether you have made the move to the cloud or not, there are reasonable security options available, but mere software and automated processes are not enough. While software and automated processes are a sensible first step, a virus/malware protector is only a partial solution. Currently, there are many cost-efficient options for Cloud Security available directly from your cloud services provider or a third-party cloud services. However, it is my firm belief that in order to protect yourself and your business against myriad cyber threats, you need to employ cutting edge technology in tandem with a set of targeted processes and protocols religiously followed by the human element. Once again, the human element is absolutely necessary. While software may be able to monitor for oncoming attacks, it takes an expert in the field of IT security to recognize the small clues indicating a larger potential breach.

Points of Interest:

1. The more confidential data we store on our computers, the more temptation we are putting in front of a hacker's face.
2. One of the easiest ways for a hacker to steal your information is by your unknowingly giving it to them.
3. No one can know every hacker game. Think in basic terms and address each piece of connected manufactured equipment. Take the time to reset all passwords using a phrase word generator.
4. Education and teamwork are key to online security and privacy.
5. Avoid complacency through coordinated refreshers and drills.

Nothing happens without the Human Element

In GROUNDING THE CLOUD: BASICS AND BROKERAGES we spent a great deal of time discussing the human element. The human element is the abilities, expectations, and personalities that affect organizations. Oftentimes people attempting to apply technology to their business greatly overlook the human element. As the case may be, the same is holding true for big data and cyber-security. In a time when we are hearing more about machine learning and artificial intelligence, it is assumed that our computers and devices will become more powerful. The real question is whether they will become wiser. Not without the human element. We will atrophy if we adopt Machine to Machine (M2M) and autonomous machine learning as our ultimate goal. As of late we have seen some high-profile examples of what can and will go wrong when we let technology take the lead (Target, Sony, OPM, Yahoo, the 2016 Presidential campaign...) These occurrences didn't have to happen.

Simply put, computers are not a panacea. They can't fix problems they don't know about, which means the human element is indispensable. Regardless of how strong or powerful our computers become, humans in leadership positions will always be necessary to teach the computers what to do, what to look for, when and how to respond, etc.

I am not taking the stand that if we let machines have more control, the movie THE TERMINATOR is bound to come true. However, how smart do we want our devices to be? More importantly, how smart are they capable of becoming?

As human beings, we have inputted and stored more data in the past several years than in all of history. We did this with help of massive computers utilizing complicated algorithms, giving birth to big data and all of its benefits. This is a very powerful thing.

Big data has the potential to help all of mankind in myriad ways. Diseases can be cured, global warming can be exposed, extinction of animals can be reduced and the world's water supply may be increased. You name it and the human element is closer to finding a way to solve it, all because of big data.

All this data mining is making our computers smarter, too. Computers learn from reoccurring inputs. Computers see a pattern and start to analyze and give predictions.

The problem is that computers are inherently neutral, only knowing what we tell them, so we as human beings must remain engaged. Take the healthcare industry as an example. A patient goes to see Doctor X. The doctor assumes that his snazzy new digital medical records system is completely accurate and doesn't bother to ask the patient about any new medications or supplements he/she may be taking. See where I'm going with this? Cases just like this are occurring daily and will be just the tip of the iceberg as time goes on if we aren't careful.

This brings us to security. While we have to protect our data and our networks, we can't forget that the most important thing we need to protect is ourselves, our families, and the people we love from the technology we work with, live by, and enjoy.

As a trained risk manager, I see statistics regarding how careless individuals are when they venture into cyberspace. On a daily basis people love to login to their social networks to let everyone know where they are going to be and when, and then share with the world details of their daily interactions, complete with pictures. Many people don't even attempt to hide their personal information from the general public – their "friends" - let alone the various criminals and hackers who are swarming the internet every second of every day. And that isn't the half of it. We also browse and shop online with unfettered abandon, making ourselves open books for any and all to see. Back in the old days bad guys had to accost us to get our wallets and steal our credit cards. Now, we basically give it to them in the form of self-created peepholes in our internet privacy.

When criminals break into a system that lets them steal our identity and max out our credit cards, we blame the hackers or poor on-line security, but the fact is *for those who haven't already done so* there are simple, common sense steps that we can take to prevent the breach in the first place. Just as we lock our doors at night in the "real world," we can put a lock on our digital profile.

- Always verify that your connection is secure as indicated by the little padlock in your browser bar and/or by looking for HTTPS:// as opposed to HTTP:// at the beginning of your intended web address.
- It's highly recommended to consolidate your cyber tools, especially if you are going to buy online as most of us do. Have a dedicated email address solely for e-commerce and isolate your electronic payment method by way of a dedicated credit card. Even better, begin using an electronic option such as PayPal, Apple Pay, or Amazon Payments.
- Clean up your cyber footprint. Get a copy of your credit report* and use this as your foundation to correct any incorrect information regarding past delinquencies and closed accounts. Close any and all social media services that you don't use, and think twice about how much personal information you want to share with anyone on any platform.
- Use a password generator, and stop using the same weak password; 12345, your middle name or a child's birthday.
- Dashlane.com and Keepass.info offer free password generators and online password vaults that are very effective in protecting you and your personal information from the point of login.
- Use plenty of caution. Be proactive when browsing the net as some pages (porn, music, file-sharing sites, etc.) are more apt than others to have spyware, malware and/or hackers lurking about. Consider taking advantage of free anti-malware and/or anti-virus programs from Microsoft, Malwarebytes, or AVG.

Learn how to control your cookie intake by adjusting your security-related Internet settings.

- Heed warnings. Security related pop-ups occur for a reason. Don't give out personally identifiable information too easily. Just as you might think twice about giving a clerk at the mall your home address and phone number, keep in mind that simply because a site asks for or demands personal information from you does not mean you have to comply.
- Don't engage. We have all been told, "If you don't have anything nice to say…" That old adage most definitely applies to the Internet, with the emphasis shifting to written speech instead of spoken words. Point is, if you don't have anything nice to write, don't. Don't engage in blogs, chat sessions or other forums where misinformation, hate or other malicious endeavors may be the intent. Deescalate. If you think what you are doing is hurtful, it probably is. Never lash out or try to hurt another's feelings with your comments online because the simple fact is, your written words never go away once posted. They're trackable and traceable forever, like a trail of breadcrumbs that can lead back to YOU months or years after you no longer care or feel differently about the subject or person.
- Read the Terms of Use and Privacy Agreements. All social networks and ecommerce sites have Terms of Use and Privacy Agreements. Don't be shy about not signing up for a site because you don't like how they may expose you. Many sites can and do commoditize your data. The only hope that your information won't be sold is if you are paying for the site or service and even then they may sell you out. Set your accounts to their highest privacy settings. There are a lot of bad people out there. The more streamlined your movement, the safer you and your personal information will be.
- Don't <u>ever</u> pay for your credit report. Don't be fooled by companies including freecreditreport.com et al, whose main

interest is to sign you up for an expensive monthly "monitoring" service. The following link is the only page to visit for a truly FREE annual credit report: HYPERLINK "https://www.annualcreditreport.com/requestReport/landingPage.action" https://www.annualcreditreport.com/requestReport/landingPage.action

- AnnualCreditReport.com was established by the federal government to comply with the Fair and Accurate Credit Transactions Act (FACT Act), legislation that requires credit bureaus to provide consumers with a copy of their credit report once a year. It is the only **official** site you should use to obtain a FREE copy of your credit report from Experian, TransUnion, Equifax, or all three.

Points of Interest:

1. The human element is the abilities, capabilities and personalities that affect organizations.
2. Computers are not a panacea; the human element will always be necessary.
3. Isolate email and electronic payment methods.
4. Use a password phrase generator.
5. Be judicious about sharing any of your personal information online.

Real World

Proctor & Gamble

Bob Herbold's career is a veritable timeline for the rise of big data over the last half century. In the late 1960's, Bob joined Proctor & Gamble fresh out of graduate school. At his new job with P&G, already the world's largest consumer products company, Bob worked primarily in research and development, simulating chemical reactions on digital computers. Bob was a fast learner, and after a few years in the trenches he was in charge of the R&D computing center. Little did he know his life was about to change in a major way when he was asked to relocate to the home office in Cincinnati, Ohio where he was given responsibility for P&G's corporate data center and global telecom network.

The leaders at P&G were early adopters of computer technology and quick to recognize the importance of customer feedback. In his new assignment, Bob was working with huge databases and mining data before there was such a thing as big data or data analytics. In those days it was simply viewed as data. By performing a microcosmic version of what big data projects provide today, Bob's team was able to gain valuable insight into the likes, dislikes, and general buying habits of their customers, including the all-important physical demographic. Even this small cross section of relevant data, interpreted properly, was enabling P&G to stay well ahead of their competition. All of this data was being collected, interpreted and secured under Bob's watch.

In 1974, Bob was asked to move into brand management and marketing. He was reluctant at first; however, within a short time Bob came to realize the truly quantitative nature of consumer marketing. He used the skills and knowledge gleaned from his Master's and PhD degrees in Mathematics and Computer Science from Case Western Reserve University to guide his team in their ongoing task of growing P&G's many brands. Quickly moving up the chain of command in brand management, Bob was given the assignment of VP of Market Research. This was followed by two years as the VP of all information technology and services within the company.

It was in this capacity in 1987 that Bob was asked by P&G to join a small group summoned to Bentonville, Arkansas to work with fast growing mega retailer Walmart. This small P&G team was assembled to work closely with Sam Walton and some of his top associates on a project to create a continuous stock replenishment program that would work on a scale large enough to satisfy Walmart's needs.

The dream for creating this highly streamlined system, which has come to be known as Continuous Inventory Replenishment, or CIR, started with Sam Walton himself. Years prior on a trip to Great Britain, Sam had stopped by a Marks and Spenser department store in London. Sam noticed that this store had the freshest flowers he had ever seen and asked the clerk in the cut-flowers department how they had such fresh flowers. She told Sam that the flowers were delivered fresh every morning. Sam couldn't understand such a concept, so he showered the lady with questions. Eventually he learned that at the close of the business day, clerks were making phone calls to their flower suppliers, giving detailed data on inventory movement over the past 24 hours for the product each supplier was providing. The suppliers then prepared the replenishment order that provided just the right amount of what would be needed over the next 24 hours and delivered that product the next morning before the store opened.

To be sure, Sam Walton was no stranger to the rigors of inventory replenishment, having grown a single Ben Franklin variety store into a successful chain of more than a dozen between 1945 and 1955. Already well aware of the value of delegating authority to build a successful entity, Sam knew there had to be a better way than for individual departments to spend valuable man-hours making phone calls to vendors. Given Walmart's size, he would need to completely automate what he'd seen at Marks and Spencer. The dawn of the computer age couldn't happen soon enough for Sam Walton, and by the late 1980s the technology was available to make his dream a reality. Walmart chose their largest supplier, Proctor & Gamble, to lead the way. Sam wanted P&G to automate the process, which necessitated the creation of entirely new software specifically for Walmart, a daunting task. Bob left the meeting excited for the opportunity.

Back at P&G, Bob and his team quickly rose to the challenge. As envisioned, this automatic, continuous inventory replenishment system would use algorithms to track the movement of P&G brands at each Walmart location for the previous 24 hours and transmit it directly to P&G's computing center. This in turn prompted P&G's distribution center to deliver the proper amount – no more, no less - of P&G products to Walmart stores in order to maintain fully stocked shelves storewide. Sam Walton's goal was to never see empty shelves, to never be sold out of a given product, and daily fulfillment would enable both Walmart and their vendors to maximize inventory. An ancillary benefit of this new system enabled Walmart to drastically reduce the number of buyers used to deal with P&G brands, which in turn enabled P&G to reduce the size of its sales force that called on those buyers.

When the P&G team went back to Walmart to show the results of their work, Sam was thrilled. In a little over ten weeks their system was up and running, testing Sam's concept on Pampers® baby diapers, one of P&G's best-selling products. It was a wildly successful experiment, cutting inventories for both companies and increasing the speed of movement from P&G to Walmart to the consumer, all with a minimum of involvement from P&G sales or Walmart buyers. Soon after all of P&G's brands were moved onto the system, Walmart began requiring other vendors to implement Continuous Inventory Replenishment. Before long, Walmart was not just requesting, but requiring, 100% of their vendors to participate in the CIR system.

Fresh off this success, in 1989 Bob took on the role of senior vice president of advertising and information services, a rather unique combination of two responsibilities. First, Bob was responsible for managing P&G's brand and marketing operations as well as marketing and retail promotion related services worldwide. Second, he was responsible for all the worldwide information technology and market research activities.

In 1994, after twenty-six years of service to Proctor & Gamble and many successes, Bob Herbold accepted a request to fly to Redmond, Washington and spent a day chatting with Bill Gates. Bob enjoyed the conversation and apparently Bill did as well, because a few days later Bob had an offer to become the Chief Operating Officer at Microsoft, a position he would enjoy for seven years, retiring in 2001. He then worked part-time for Microsoft for two more years as an Executive VP, helping Bill and Steve Ballmer with customer, industry, and government relations issues. During Bob's time at Microsoft, there was a four-fold increase in revenue and a seven-fold increase in profit, and employment tripled. He is now Managing Director of the Herbold Group, a consulting firm that assists individuals and organizations with improving their performance in areas of strategy and profitability.

As Bob reflects on his fascinating journey, it reminds us that technology is constantly changing the work place. Today more than ever, information is the battlefront, and big data is the tip of the sword. Many successful companies have come to realize the true power and potential residing in large databases, and those on the cutting edge will continue to take advantage of the increasing speed of servers along with the sophistication of new algorithms to increase their bottom line. Any organization currently dependent on human hands, with our individual work ethics and energy levels, will continue to automate every process possible. The final step, however, will always require the human touch. While the mining of data is not a new concept, it continues to be the human element *combined* with advancing technology that has proven invaluable in developing immediate responses to real time occurrences.

Points of Interest:

1. According to Bob Herbold, "Big Data is the smart use of databases to determine trends and behaviors that suggest certain actions that will be beneficial."
2. Big data is not a new concept. Bob Herbold and Procter & Gamble were data mining and developing automated solutions in the 1970s.
3. Information is the battlefront, and big data is the tip of the sword.
4. The growth of automated responses in real time driven by big data is proving invaluable.
5. Ultimate accountability will always fall on an organization's human element. Therefore, organizational success remains dependent on individual leadership of diverse teams to develop and implement new technology.

DineEquity

In 2007, famous pancake purveyors IHOP bought bar & grill chain Applebee's, turning the company now called DineEquity into one of the nation's largest sit-down restaurant chains by locations and sales, with a total of over 3,800 locations. In the spring of 2010, Executive Director of Human Resources Dan Block walked into his office at DineEquity's Glendale, California headquarters as a man on a mission. His task? Combining the operational environments of Applebee's and IHOP, which to this point had been run separately using totally different systems, into a single corporate culture. DineEquity's board wanted to oversee one company with multiple brands instead of operating two separate restaurant chains. It was the biggest technological human resources project of Dan's career and the jobs of more than a quarter million people depended on his getting it right.

The end goal wasn't just to combine and streamline technology. DineEquity was expecting increased human productivity across the board. It was going to take multiple initiatives across numerous work environments and Dan knew instinctively that revamped ERP software was where he had to begin. ERP, short for *enterprise resource planning,* is business management HYPERLINK "http://www.webopedia.com/TERM/S/software.html" software that uses a system of HYPERLINK "http://www.webopedia.com/TERM/I/integrated.html" integrated applications to manage all facets of an operation, including product planning, development, manufacturing, sales and marketing, and of course human resources.

Dan's immediate need was to find a company to create customized software. When new ERP software is created, there is a certain amount of off-the-shelf technology utilized, but DineEquity needed industry-specific customization in the end product. As opposed to a one-size-fits-all "template" solution, Dan wanted a firm to come in to analyze the systems that were currently in place at Applebee's and IHOP, come up with a list of best practices from both and then write new integrated software that preserved what worked well from each current system. The goal for the new entity was to enhance the work culture and overall productivity while *not* requiring every employee to learn a totally new system.

Having been the International Human Resources Director with Applebee's when they were purchased by IHOP, and having served in a similar position with Microsoft prior to that, Dan was well aware of the enormity of the task before him. He understood the very diverse workforce(s) he was dealing with. Each location had dozens of employees, from dishwashers and cooks to wait staff, hosts, and managers. They were mostly young. Many did not possess technical skills and not all spoke English as a first language, so ease of use in this new ERP system was absolutely paramount.

Dan was also aware of the high turnover rate in the restaurant industry and the need to keep "filling the funnel" with new hires. It was a daunting task. Homogenizing the cultures of both chains, made that much more difficult because of his chief mandate: keeping as much as possible from the current processes and systems. It simply wasn't feasible to install an all-new IT system from the ground up in 3000+ restaurants.

At the time, DineEquity was running PeopleSoft ERP. While PeopleSoft is one of the oldest and more trusted names in the industry, going forward it was not turning out to be the best fit for DineEquity. First of all, it was very expensive, costing DineEquity over $1.2 million dollars a year. PeopleSoft had limited flexibility in their payment offerings and they charged per user, which was already a problem for DineEquity. It was going to be an even larger problem in the near future as they were about to embark on selling locations to franchisees and numerous employees were going to begin to drop off rapidly. DineEquity would soon be paying for lots of software space that they weren't using if they continued usage of PeopleSoft.

Dan had to find an ERP provider that understood his highest priority was catering to the human element, noting that software providers in general need to recognize that not everyone works in a cubicle or has technical skills. After thorough research Dan contacted Ultimate Software, headquartered in Weston, Florida with offices in Toronto, Canada, based in large part on the fact that Ultimate offered to send out usability teams to multiple restaurant locations in order to learn about the different types of users and work environments that Applebee's and IHOP employees were experiencing.

While Ultimate Software worked to analyze the current system(s) in order to custom configure their ERP SaaS product, Dan pivoted to another major issue he'd been monitoring: the drop-off in DineEquity's completed job applications. On average after eight minutes, 50% of applicants had stopped filling out the application. For an industry with high turnover, that is not a good thing. Dan needed to figure out a way to increase the completion level on their applications, so he hit the data. It turned out that people under the age of 25 wanted a gamification approach on job applications. Gone are the days of using pens and a piece of paper on a clipboard to apply for a job. The new generation was losing interest quickly and not completing the applications. Not only would the application itself have to be updated, but the process of applying would have to change. The new way would need to be in a format engaging to the eye and of interest to the age, including the option of an immediate download of the applicant's current resume/work history from either a MS Word file or a networking site such as LinkedIn, Monster, CareerBuilder, et al. This would not be a one-size-fits-all solution as the average 20-year-old wanted a shopping cart type of job application, and the 40-50-year- old manager type wanted a typical ERP type interface job application.

Dan decided that the key to obtaining more completed job applications and thus more employees was offering multiple options in the application process. One application can't possibly meet the needs of every person. That is not how the human element works. For technology to help productivity, the workforce needs to be engaged, and that engagement begins with the initial job application. Dan believed that a world- class company such as DineEquity should offer a "pick your experience" type of job application. The reason this isn't typically accomplished is that software developers tend to be rather inflexible. As a group they don't embrace change - methodology changes or platform changes. Ultimate Software, on the other hand, was proving to be more than capable of rising to Dan's challenge. The new job application was adopted by the board and with an average completion time of six minutes, drop-off rates dwindled significantly.

Dan was pleased with the overall implementation of Ultimate Software's solution, as was DineEquity's senior leadership. The move consolidated many of their systems, not only making things easier on management but also employees and even more importantly, it saved the company a lot of money.

While everyone seemed happy with Ultimate Software and their ERP system, Dan also had to ensure the security of the new system. He knew that there was no way that DineEquity could cost effectively keep their on-premises servers more secure or safer than a cloud services provider (CSP). Understanding the company was not equipped to deal with this challenge on their own meant one thing: DineEquity was ready to move to the cloud.

DineEquity moved to the cloud (or in lay speak, shut down their internal data centers) and all of DineEquity's data and servers now sit with private and hybrid cloud services provider TierPoint (formerly Cosentry). Ultimate has always been a Software-as-a-Service (SaaS) product and as such they maintain their own server farm. As a restaurant company, DineEquity did not want to also be an IT company, thus their strategic outsourcing of network and software.

The one disappointment that Dan had in Ultimate Software was something that every ERP system had yet to figure out – the lack of security in protecting sensitive company data from potential interlopers outside as well as inside the operation. There was always the opportunity for an employee to sneak in and steal data, social security numbers, protected health information (PHI) in the form of drug tests, insurance claims, all that could end up in identity theft or worse.

While Dan had a great deal of appreciation for the rising field of Big Data, he was wondering how the ERP systems and other data gathering software systems were going to protect their end users to the fullest extent. Dan had several ideas on the matter. As a former employee of Microsoft, he recalled having to use an employee badge to turn his computer on, a good first step in the front line for internal security. At least you would know who compromised the data, but you could never stop that person from making a copy of the hard drive. Dan then remembered back to 1994 when he worked at Gateway. They'd produced a PC for their employees without floppy disk or CD drives that also required a key card for login. At the time this was the most secure machine on the market for employee use.

In concert with TierPoint's risk management initiatives and through the use of IBM Cognos Analytics (security suite enable) compounded with extensive data masking, DineEquity and Ultimate felt that employees were effectively blocked from viewing and barred from downloading certain fields such as social security numbers.

Dan realized that he would not be the one to figure out the ultimate solution to the security issues with ERP systems or Big Data. He was, however, the one who put together a very good solution for DineEquity and that was enough for him...for then.

Points of Interest:

1. What is an ERP? Enterprise resource planning is business management software that uses a system of integrated applications to manage all facets of an operation, including product planning, development, manufacturing, sales and marketing, and of course human resources. A company's ERP system holds some of its most priceless assets, its data.
2. Employee data should be treated as proprietary company data.
3. Cloud services such as Ultimate Software and TierPoint provide mobility and scalability.

4. There are always internal security concerns with ERP systems and employee breaches.
5. It is up to individual companies to set and monitor parameters and internal system permissions to help ensure that employee and business data stays secure.

Hewlett Packard Enterprise

Few people in the country are as knowledgeable in the field of cyber-security as Logan Browne. At the age of 23 he was working at Hewlett-Packard doing security analysis. A few years later he switched over to vulnerability analysis, and before he was 30-years old he took on a role in forensics and investigations. Logan moved up the ladder in a variety of management positions before accepting his current position as the Director and Chief Technologist of Hewlett Packard Enterprise's Global Cyber Security.

Today, Logan oversees 200 employees and under his direction they monitor the internal cyber-security of HPE. Logan's division is also responsible for protecting the data of approximately 400,000+ employees, including their business, technical, and consumer data.

It is almost unfathomable how many times each day HPE comes under attack from outside entities. The key to handling these attacks is gathering all of the different security events logged by various firewalls and intrusion prevention systems into a centralized security, management and prevention system. Most of this can be done with adaptive cyber-security software such as HPE's ArcSight. Much like the U.S. government monitors potential military attacks from NORAD's fortified command & control center, ArcSight assembles data on all of the attacks from systems and machines across HPE's vast array of worldwide networks and collates that information into a central hub where Logan's team of security analysts examine data, make decisions and take appropriate action in real-time.

HPE ArcSight DNS Malware Analytics applies many security precautions including a passive DNS query logging and analysis to protect against unknown attacks. This eliminates chasing ghosts in the machine. Logan believes that by examining the proper data, a highly adaptive security system can actually prevent attacks from occurring. HPE is focused on moving away from traditional reactive security and towards predictive, adaptive security solutions.

After working for three years with HP's advanced lab at Princeton and a year and a half with the ArcSight group, Logan and his team developed Haven™, one of HPE's newest software in the security realm. Haven actively looks for "bad behavior" in the system by detecting patterns which indicate that attacks large or small may be imminent.

When a potential breach is indicated, Haven gathers information from several sources while shutting down the appropriate sector(s). Haven provides an array of intelligent security responses which are then evaluated and implemented by the human element.

Utilizing Haven, Logan's team was able to detect hackers that were on a mission to slowly break into HPE's system over a three-month period of time. Haven was able to identify the patterns of attack and shut them down before data was stolen or a virus inserted. In being proactive, HPE was able to thwart the attack instead of picking up the pieces afterwards.

But sometimes the attackers aren't on the outside. Sometimes they come from the inside in the form of your own employees. Protecting your internal security apparatus can be even more problematic than guarding from external threats. The problem is two-fold and includes the dishonest or compromised employee who purposely attempts to bypass security measures, as well as the inept or inexperienced worker who may inadvertently expose your data to thieves and hackers. Ultimately, the best defense is to separate and compartmentalize systems, i.e. employees working at their desk need separation from the servers at the data center, which should be separate from the information processing of consumer credit card information.

In an effort toward minimizing potential damage created by employees through ill will and/or operator error, Logan advocates presenting numerous hurdles as the best way to protect and secure valuable assets. Forward leaning companies including HPE are driving towards more segmentation in their IT and security systems. Some organizations separate accessibility by departments, some by functions. Regardless of these specific delineations, all companies should have protocols that limit open file sharing in order to guard against viruses, malware, phishing scams, etc.

One of the trickiest issues to deal with is something called lateral movement. This is the most difficult problem to catch. Attackers compromise an employee user-ID account and use these "authorized" credentials to move throughout an organization.

What makes this so hard to catch is that it is an authorized ID and looks like an employee moving around the company doing normal work. A security system needs significant layers of monitoring to catch this type of attack. HPE has systems in place to detect anomalous behavior and lateral movements inside the company which combat attackers who are using stolen credentials.

Cyber-attacks come fast and furious; there is often little or no time for the human element to be involved in the initial tactical response. The best line of defense is one that is highly automated. Security analysts must be on staff for oversight and implementation of additional measures. Upon detection of a potential breach, the system should be designed to protect itself on the spot by limiting access or shutting down while simultaneously alerting its human counterparts.

Every day, the Cyber-security team at Hewlett Packard Enterprise is hard at work, and Logan is in constant communication with IT companies and various technologists following the newest trends and keeping up on the most cutting-edge security measures. As data becomes more valuable, hackers and the methods they use are becoming more sophisticated. The battlefield is in a constant state of flux, forcing IT security teams to become exponentially more inventive. No matter what the future brings in cyber-security, it is a given that Logan Browne and HPE will be at the forefront in creating technology that keeps our critical assets and most sensitive data safe and secure.

Points of Interest:

1. The key to defending against cyber-attacks is to centralize actionable intelligence in your command and control center.
2. Much like maintaining other elements of your IT infrastructure, your security measures require proactivity and the appropriate budget.
3. The security measures taken to protect your business internally are more challenging than preventing security breaches from external threats.
4. The best way to protect against internal threats is to separate and compartmentalize your IT systems and functions.
5. Regardless of how capable the technologies to defend against security threats are, you still need the analysts and the IT people – the human element.

University of Maryland University College

"Fifteen years ago two planes ran into the Twin Towers. More recently a bomb was detonated in a crowd of thousands at the finish line of the Boston Marathon. In today's society we picture terrorists wielding AK-47's and planting bombs. While this has been true in the past it is changing, and changing quickly." William McBourrough had the full attention of his audience as he continued his lecture to students in this cyberterrorism course at the University of Maryland University College (UMUC). "Many terrorists are no longer carrying weapons; instead they are sitting in front of a computer hammering on a keyboard, planning and implementing attacks on our government, our largest corporations, and even places of care such as hospitals and related insurance networks. These cyber- terrorists can attack at any time without warning from the comfort of their own home and home country. Before long the terrorists won't need to be on a plane in order to crash them into buildings, they will be able to fly the planes anywhere they want with several lines of code." Welcome to the modern age of cyber warfare.

William is an Adjunct Professor, teaching multiple courses in the cyber-security undergraduate degree program at UMUC including: cybercrime, cyber-terrorism, systems and telecommunications security architecture, information security assessment and planning, information security policy and ethical hacking.

William had been studying and working in the field of security for over fifteen years, long before there was the field of cyber-security. He has designed, built and managed security systems and programs in various sectors including financial services, health care, national service, state government, and higher education, consistently speaking out about the dangers of cyber-terrorism and what was coming down the pipeline. Just a few years ago, not many foresaw the day when the simple act of using a credit card would put you at risk of becoming a victim - but William did.

William attended George Mason University, minutes away from the heart of Washington D.C. He majored in computer engineering and digital networks and went on to receive a Master's in Information Security and Assurance. Living and going to school in the capital, William was exposed to the world of national security and quickly became aware of the high importance for risk management and proactive solutions to cybersecurity. In William's view, everyone – individuals, companies, and especially the government - must have a line of defense in their IT protocol.

In 2010, William founded the SMB Cyber Security Alliance, a volunteer-run organization created to bring awareness to small business owners about the necessity of privacy, security and protection in the digital age and provide options for companies to take personal responsibility for their own security.

Not long after, William joined the Department of Homeland Security's Transportation Security Administration (TSA) as a Contract Project Manager doing Security Architecture. William managed the program that helped to provide a secure infrastructure and subject matter expertise, security testing and security audit testing. TSA has changed a lot from the pre-technology era to today.

Nowadays, TSA needs an entire division devoted to protecting IT surrounding the airlines and anything to do with air travel. The security architecture built around this system needs to be bullet proof and needs eyes on it at all times. As technology develops, the people behind the attacks are able to be more destructive.

In addition to teaching at UMUC, currently William is also the Co-Founder and managing Principal at Mission Critical Global Technology Group (MCGlobalTech). MCGlobalTech is an information security consulting firm that helps clients manage their cyber-security risks and defend against cyber threats and attacks. William founded MCGlobalTech in 2013 because he saw the increased need in the private small business arena for increased IT infrastructure security.

The first things William teaches every organization is that their data is their biggest asset and it is up to them to decide how much they want to protect their assets. While it is up to a company if they choose to protect their assets or not, it is most certainly their fiduciary responsibility to protect their clients' and employees' data.

William works with many organizations that don't have the right to choose how they safeguard their data. There are some highly compliant industries that have rules and regulations to follow as it pertains to protecting their data - industries such as health care, law firms, and financial institutions.

Several years ago William was brought on board to consult for an up and coming financial company that wanted to move to the cloud. This company was a startup and needed the cost savings and all the added benefits the cloud would bring them. William researched, prepared and ranked a list of possible cloud services providers and his client chose one. While William accepted his client's final decision he could not fully endorse their move forward with the public cloud even though it was the most cost effective approach. Instead he highly recommended they choose a private cloud offering because at the time the public cloud could not offer a secure enough network.

Today, moving to a cloud environment is a red-hot topic, as is security and risk management. Hence, this is where William spends a lot of time researching and addressing options with clients. The best advice William has to offer is: "As an organization you place a certain value on your assets and data. You decide how much time and money you want to invest in case your server goes down or your data gets corrupted. On the other hand, if you move to the cloud and mitigate some of those risks, you are putting your data in the hands of a cloud services provider.

Daunting as it may be, always read the Service Level Agreements. Thoroughly understand how they are managing, utilizing and protecting your data and information. Ask questions! Think responsibly and make intelligent decisions, not just for your company but also for your employees and customers."

As technology marches forward we are seeing less reasons to fear the cloud. The options are becoming more obvious and if caution is observed there is no reason not to continue the migration. For what it's worth, the Central Intelligence Agency (CIA) uses public cloud services offered by Amazon Web Services (AWS).

More recently William has been consulting with Homeland Security on how to bring together twenty-plus agencies with multiple IT infrastructures. The shared services initiative seeks to consolidate the IT of the over 20 departments into a single cloud environment with everyone working on the same platform (e.g. Microsoft Azure, Microsoft business tools.) Due to the evolving quality of services being offered, this has been a challenging process. There are no one size fits all solution, yet there are technological silos such as email and file sharing that can fulfill a large portion of an organization's IT needs.

Despite the cyber-security challenges we are facing today and those coming down the pike tomorrow, William believes that being alert and armed with knowledge, organizations can be on a secure footing while realizing the benefits of utilizing the public cloud and big data.

Points of Interest:

1. Your data is your biggest asset and it is up to you to decide how you want to protect it.
2. Certain industries are required to have measurable standards and protocols in place for express IT security measures.
3. Read a cloud service providers end user license agreement and/or service level agreements thoroughly. Don't assume security measures are being provided for you.
4. The recognition that data is valuable has increased data poaching.
5. With education and alertness, organizations can be prepared and avoid security lapse.

Next Steps

Your Security and Big-Data Checklists:

SECURITY

1. How is your executive leadership informed about the current level and business impact of cyber risks to our company?
2. What is the current level and business impact of cyber risks to your company?
3. What is your plan to address identified risks?
4. How does your cyber-security program apply industry standards and best practices?
5. How many and what types of cyber incidents do you detect in an average week?
6. What is the threshold for notifying your executive leadership?
7. How comprehensive is your cyber incident response plan?
8. How often is it tested?
9. What does your security look like?
10. What does your security program look like?
11. What are your security requirements?
12. Assess your risk.
13. Assess your controls.
14. Assess your data assets.
15. What data is critical to you?
16. What happens if there is a leak?
17. What if a cloud services provider has access to your data?
18. What additional controls do you need to put in place?
19. How do you make sure your cloud services provider is meeting your security needs?
20. What type of internal security do you need?
21. What type of external security do you need?
22. What type of privacy do you need for your employees?

23. What type of privacy measures do you take for yourself on social media?
24. Are you using a complex password?
25. Are you using a password phrase generator?
26. Does your organization properly encrypt proprietary data?

Big Data

1. Big data – what is it you want to know?
2. Do you have a "big data" challenge or a "lots of data" challenge?
3. Where will the data come from?
4. Is it worth it?
5. What is your budget?
6. Will it work?
7. What are most pressing challenges in your business?
8. With better insights and information, how could you overcome challenges and improve your bottom line?
9. How will you get to know your customers better?
10. How can you apply these insights and manage them to cash in on the opportunity that big data has presented?
11. What is the price you pay for your software?
12. Does size matter?
13. Where is your data?
14. What is the right data you need to grow your business?
15. What data can you extract to excite your customers and gain a competitive edge?
16. Can you find the 80/20 analytics that matter?
17. Do you have a qualified employee to work with the data?
18. How ethical and transparent is your data collection?
19. Did you violate anyone's privacy to get your data?
20. Are you prepared for bad news?
21. How is your company treated online?
22. How do you treat others online?

23. What is the cost of sitting on the fence and not moving forward?
24. Does your data have any legal ramifications?
25. Big Data and Hadoop – what do they mean?
26. What is the reality of implementation?
27. When is the right time for implementation?
28. How does big data fit into your culture?
29. How much money do you want to spend on big data?
30. How much time do you have to implement a big data project?
31. Which departments should be involved?
32. Can you use the cloud or do you reside on premise?
33. What data do you want to capture?
34. How long do you want to store your data?
35. Who should be the sponsor of the big data project?

Create a Big Data Plan

Company managers and owners are looking for the best way to jump on the biggest trend of today: big data. The majority of companies don't have the options that the big boys do of bringing on data scientists and analysts, or even utilizing highly functional software aka expensive software. But that doesn't mean you aren't able to start using your data to your benefit for little or even no money. Remember, you need to know what you think you are looking for. I have compiled a list of some of my favorite options for getting your business into the big data game right away, if you decide to do so.

My first choice is IBM's Watson Analytics. It offers advanced analytics while still being simple to use, an excellent option for businesses without employees skilled in reading analytics. My favorite thing about this option, other than being free, is that it is a software-as-a-service. Yes, it is cloud based, something I favor. Watson Analytics easily integrates your data into the software, undergoes its data exploration, automates predictive analytics and reports results on a simple-to-read dashboard. You are handed the detailed reports and new insights to make confident decisions in minutes—all on your own.

There is a specific analytic system for your IT, marketing, finance, sales, operations, and HR department to improve all your business needs.

Canopy Labs is my next choice. It has many similar features to IBM's Watson Analytics but for those grasping to have a physical ownership, it is a downloadable software.

There is a free option with Canopy Labs, but, it doesn't hold a candle to free Watson. You get what you pay for. A useful tool involves payment. Billing is based on the number of customers. I would recommend this data analytics solution for a slightly larger small business.

With Canopy Labs you are able to see how every marketing and sales channel impacts the decisions your customers make, from website visits, email clicks, demographics, website and in-store purchases. There are built-in automated marketing messages, product recommendations, personalized content delivered to email, and offers based on customer activity and predictions.

After your initial setup with Canopy Labs, the views and reports update automatically. The system will analyze your past data and will continue processing your future data. All of the predictions are made within the platform and can be exported to other platforms.

There are companies that don't even have enough data to warrant the need for big data software, but would like the prestige that big data offers. There is a solution out there, for them, too. And it starts by getting more data from their customers. It may sound like a daunting task but with all of the available software out there, it doesn't have to be. One of the best solutions to getting more information is very easy: The Survey. Most people only consider surveys when thinking about Facebook. But we all get them and with appropriate incentive, many of us fill them out. The software solution that I recommend to get meaningful data on your customers is Qualtrics.

Qualtrics is a leading enterprise survey platform. It offers several different types of targeted surveys. Surveys have never been easier; companies can find customers' insights online.

Qualtrics customizable surveys allow you to hear firsthand what your customers have to say to you, while the widespread reach that Qualtrics has into social media allows you to find out what your customers are saying to each other.

Qualtrics allows you to gather a full picture of data, more than what you may already have in your arsenal. That is what I like so much about this service.

There's more: Qualtrics Research Suite software and Site Intercept analyzes the data and then makes it easier to predict what your customers will do and captures the data from your website visitors, respectively. With all of the options available from Qualtrics you will surely be satisfied.

With the all the options available to integrate data analysis into your business, you will surely be able to find a way to manage and utilize your data in no time.

Points of Interest:

1. Understand what you are hoping to learn as you enter the big data space.
2. Do you know how much data you really have? Do you need more data? Most big data products are built to handle terabytes of data.
3. Decide if you prefer a downloadable software or a SaaS.
4. Do you have an expert on your team in data analysis or do you need a software that is capable of providing easy-to-read answers for you?
5. Be sure to choose a product or service that suits your needs at this moment.

Create a Security Plan

With the exponential increase of security breaches followed by 24/7 media exploitation, we are desensitized and almost accept hacker intrusions as common place. Then it happens to you and you have to reseed your financial pasture as a result of the exposure. These new-age thieves come in and steal more than your merchandise. They steal your most important asset, the thing that you have worked the hardest for: your customers. They steal their data and their trust. It has become imperative to take additional precautions to protect our hardware, software, intellectual property, and above all, our customers' data. Once you have been hacked you have to regain their trust. But you can take additional precautions without having an entire IT and security team monitoring your IT systems. There are several security software solutions available for small businesses that assist in putting the security protocols in place so you can continue doing business with peace of mind.

One of my first suggestions is for Amazon Web Services (AWS) cloud consumers. It is Dome9 SecOps for AWS. While AWS offers several security protocols within their cloud building blocks directly, there are limited safeguards against unauthorized users modifying your console. Dome9 allows you to centrally manage all of your AWS EC2 and VPC Security Groups across multiple AWS accounts, allowing some users access to instances while restricting them from other security groups. It automatically reverts unauthorized policy changes so security is always enforced. Dome9 requires IT personnel to run and manage, but it is worth the effort and cost of $299-$599/month. This additional backup on the AWS cloud protects from both internal and external security breaches.

My next choice is a completely different type of option. It is a downloadable software called Bitedefender. Bitefender Small Business secures file servers, PC's Macs and Android devices. This is a great choice for businesses that don't have a large IT firm and don't have a large budget. While it is a powerful security option, it can only protect up to 20 devices before you need to jump to the more expensive enterprise solution. If you can stick to twenty devices or below, this is my choice for micro or small businesses for Internet security and data loss.

My third choice is also a downloadable software for small businesses, Kaspersky Lab for small office. It is reasonably priced and easy to install. It provides anti-virus, internet security and data loss just like Bitefinder does. Both Kaspersky and Bitefinder are comprehensive tools that do a great job defending against malware and attacks.

Kaspersky, however, can only support 10 workstations and is for Windows-based PC's file servers only.

My final choice is Carbonite. Carbonite provides both cloud and hybrid backup plans. I am always fond of products that integrate with the cloud. Carbonite has leveraged the power of the cloud which allows for rapid recovery anytime providing access from anywhere. Whether it's business or personal, your data is here to stay. Carbonite gives complete protection in a centralized monitoring dashboard. Best of all, if your data requires high standards of compliance, you have no need to worry: Carbonite is HIPPA, FERPA and GLBA compliant. Billing of Carbonite works in a similar way to cloud storage – you pay for your license and there are no additional licensing fees for backing up additional computers, servers or hard drives, only for the additional storage that you use. If you pay attention to the details, it doesn't get better than that.

There are many other options out there to help protect you from vicious malware, hackers and loss of data. While these are just a few of my favorites, always go with what works best with your needs and your current IT environment. The most important thing is that you choose something before someone chooses to make you their victim.

Points of Interest:

1. If you don't have a security software running on your network, add one now.
2. Never leave your computer or network unsecure. Always close down your desktop.
3. There are different products for different price ranges. Don't be alarmed if you can't afford the highest priced product.
4. Some security software will require IT personnel to run. Be sure you have these people on staff prior to purchasing this type of software.
5. Check to make sure that your security software is industry compliant.

Epilogue

In the early 1970s, I rode horses. I also showed my horse around the Delaware Valley, something I did poorly. Conversely, Mandy Weber seemed to win every time. Blue ribbon after blue ribbon, Mandy and her horse Napoleon would dominate.

Hunter/Jumper, Walk, Trot, Canter, Open Jumper, you name it, Mandy won it.

Those of us in the same class as Mandy would seek every excuse for her winning over and over, until we finally came up with one. Mandy had a "push button horse." This lack of acceptance and unwillingness to not give Mandy her do led us to our folly. It will go down in DVHS history as to who said what. However, someone said something and the next thing you know Mandy's mom is yelling, "It's only a push button horse if you know how to push the buttons." Who is to say if Mandy's mom was a "helicopter mom," or if the horse was just that perfect, but her sentiment sticks with me to this day.

Machine Learning, The Internet of Things, and Artificial intelligence are changing current day automation in both business and personal settings. In both a business and consumer environment we want everything automated right up until we realize how it has impacted us in ways we never expected.

We all want our lives to be easier, but are we willing to pay the price for simplicity? Are you willing to accept that you may be giving up your cyber-security and your cyber-privacy? Big data and security will continue to evolve and we need to take part in what is happening by staying aware and alert.

In book three: <u>Grounding the Cloud: Red, White and Shared Services</u> I go back and forth from Washington, D.C. to flyover country comparing and contrasting technology related policy. Policy that leads to processes surrounding to shared services. Speaking with subject matter experts about the bureaucratization of technology we discuss how today's Federal acquisition process is hindering taking advantage of and controlling the consumption of cloud services. This slowness is also affecting cyber-security as we hastily embrace the Internet of Things (IoT).

Acknowledgements

Thank you Jodi, Duncan and Dane.

In addition, I want to thank the following individuals for their contributions:

Brad Burke
Clifford K. Henderson
Daryl C. Plummer
John Bourisseau
Lindsay Preston
Rita Garvin
Ruthanne Myers-Fox
Sandy Barsky
Stephanie Frankiewicz

About the Author

Todd D. Lyle is a leader. Currently his focus is on educating organizations about the potential for harnessing the human element through use of the cloud via a cloud services brokerage.

His fascination with the possibilities of information technologies began when he was issued his first "laptop" while serving as a young lieutenant in a U.S. Army aviation regiment in South Korea. In 1988, a bulky Zenith SuperSport 286 portable computer was his first brush with "mobile" computing.

Years later, having served with IFOR in Bosnia as a Force Protection Officer, Lyle returned home and obtained a Master of Science in Risk Control from the University of Wisconsin – Stout in the winter of 1998. Shortly thereafter he was offered a leadership position with a major technology company. It was while working at Microsoft that Lyle became interested in utility computing commonly referred to as the cloud.

Being well aware of the potential of cloud computing, in 2007 Lyle launched Duncan Cloud Services Brokerage to participate in the development, implementation and governance of this exciting new utility. At Duncan, Lyle assembled a business and technology savvy team that created "ingenious cloud computing services bundles that focus on affordable and customer-centric solutions." *

Today Lyle draws on his military and private sector experiences to teach and talk about continuity, operations, security, and best practices when it comes to people using the internet.

Lyle's years of process development and his various wins and losses have allowed him to become a practical innovator in the realm of technology solutions. In 2013 Todd was encouraged to share "need to know technologies", the result being THE GROUNDING THE CLOUD© series.

*Gartner® Cool Vendors in Cloud Services Brokerages, 2012

Made in United States
Cleveland, OH
05 November 2026

47647250R00043